Japanese Mochi Cookbook

Explore the art of authentic Japanese Mochi

BY

Rachael Rayner

License Notes

Table of Contents

Introduction

Japanese cuisine is world famous for its uniqueness. People in Japan enjoy fast cooking but they also enjoy being artistic in the Kitchen. Mochi making is an art. You can be as creative as you want with mochi making. The simplest mochi making takes less than 10 minutes. You can add any flavors to it. Adding fresh fruits inside as stuffing is popular for mochi making.

Usually, authentic mochi makers use tapioca starch, gluttonous rice flour, corn starch, and warabi flour, to make mochi. But these starch or flour is not always available outside Japan. You can substitute these flours with potato starch. For sweetening, they use confectioner's sugar or brown sugar. You can use any type of sugar substitute if you do not eat sugar. Adding honey and agave nectar is acceptable. You will find fruits like banana, strawberries, raspberries, passionfruit, coconut etc. in the book. The diversity of ingredients is what makes this book acceptable for all types of audiences. Try these 30 delicious yet simple mochi recipes and plunge into a new cuisine.

Super Quick Milk Mochi

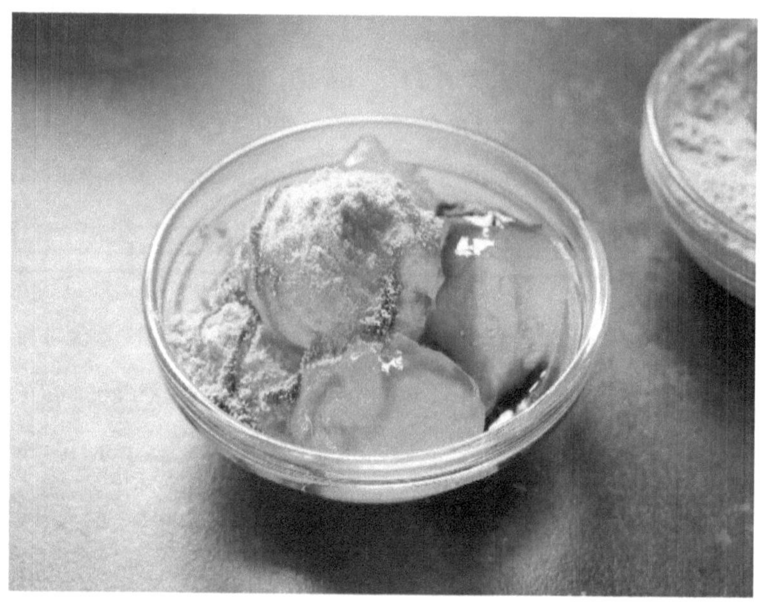

This is the most simple and quick mochi recipe out there. You can use any milk and any sweetener of your choice here.

Serving Size: 1

Cooking Time: 3 Minutes

Ingredients:

- 1/2 cup soy milk
- 2 tsp Sugar
- 2 tbsp Corn Starch
- 2 tbsp ground nuts

Instruction

In a microwave safe bowl add the soy milk.

Add the corn starch and stir until well combined

Add to the micro oven. Cook for 2 minutes.

Stir one and cook for another minute.

Add the sugar and mix well. Top with the nuts and serve in room temperature or cold.

Tofu Mochi

The Japanese love their mochi. They try every little variation available. This is a mochi made using tofu. The health value of this recipe is immense.

Serving Size: 2

Cooking Time: 20 Minutes

Ingredients:

- 300g silky soft tofu
- 100g tapioca starch
- Sweet Red bean paste to serve

Instruction

In a microwave safe bowl, add the soft tofu.

Stir until it becomes runny. Add in the tapioca starch.

Mix again for a minute. Add to the microwave. Cook for 1 minute.

Stir once and cook for another minute.

If the color changes to dark brown then it is cooked well.

Wait for it to cool down. Create little balls using your hands.

Serve cold with red bean paste on top.

Potato Cheesy Mochi

Mashed Potato is something we all make every now and then. The leftover is not that tasty the next day. You can make a fabulous mochi recipe with your leftover mashed potatoes.

Serving Size: 2

Cooking Time: 5 Minutes

Ingredients:

- 1 cup leftover mashed potato
- 1/4 cup rice flour
- 2 tbsp milk
- 1 tablespoon chopped chives
- 1 pinch of salt
- 2 tbsp grated parmesan cheese
- 1 tablespoon oil

Instruction

Combine the mashed potato with milk.

Add the chives, cheese, salt and rice flour.

Mix well. Create little balls using your hands.

Fry them golden brown with oil.

Serve.

Sweet Potato Mochi

Do you know you can enjoy a quick savory Japanese snack using sweet potatoes? It is quick to make and it looks and tastes quite good.

Serving Size: 3

Cooking Time: 5 Minutes

Ingredients:

- 1 cup sweet potato
- 1 pinch of salt
- 1/4 cup tapioca flour
- ¼ tsp mixed herbs
- Pepper to taste
- oil for frying

Instruction

Peel the sweet potatoes. Cut them coarsely.

In a pan add some oil and roast the sweet potatoes.

Use a masher to mash it finely.

Add the herbs, salt, pepper and flour.

Use your hands to knead well. Create little patties.

Fry them golden brown. Serve hot.

Mango Mochi Balls

This recipe is taking mochi making art to a different level. It looks light a fabulous sweet treat made at a good pastry shop.

Serving Size: 2

Ingredients:

- 1 cup sweet rice flour
- 1 ripe mango, cut into cubes
- ½ cup desiccated coconut
- 4 tbsp ground sugar
- 1 cup coconut milk
- 4 tbsp cornstarch
- 1 tbsp vegetable oil

Instruction

Combine the rice flour and cornstarch together.

Add the sugar and mix well.

Add the milk and oil. Make dough.

Roll out flat and take small portion of dough and create a pocket to stuff one mango cube inside. Seal the edges carefully.

Bring 2 cup of water in a pot. Drop the mochi balls. Boil for 5 minutes.

Take them out and roll the mochi balls in desiccated coconut flakes.

Serve.

Sticky Cauliflower Mochi Cakes

Adding veggies in mochi cakes give them a healthy layer. Mochi in itself tastes good but trying out different recipes with it makes mochi making a fun experience. For this recipe, I have used mashed cauliflower and it turned out quite well.

Serving Size: 2

Cooking Time: 20 Minutes

Ingredients:

- 1 cup mashed cauliflower
- Salt to taste
- 2 tbsp cornstarch
- 1 cup sticky rice flour
- 1 tbsp tapioca starch
- 3 tbsp brown sugar
- ½ cup water
- Oil for frying

Instruction

Combine the brown sugar with water. Mix well.

In a mixing bowl, add the dry ingredients.

Add the mashed cauliflower and mix well.

Add the sugar mixture and make dough.

Create small flat patties.

Fry them golden brown.

Passion Fruit Mochi

Fruit mochi are very popular because it adds the natural flavor of the fruit in a dessert.

Serving Size: 4

Cooking Time: 20 Minutes

Ingredients:

- 2 cup passion fruit juice
- 1 cup confectioner sugar
- 2 cup mochiko
- 1 cup tapioca flour

Instruction

In a bowl combine the tapioca flour with sugar.

Mix well and add the mochiko.

Mix well and add the passion fruit juice. Mix until well combined.

Place into a steamer. Steam for 20 minutes and wait for it to cool down.

Cut into squares and serve.

Lemon Mochi Ice cream

Lemon mochi ice cream has refreshing aroma and flavor to it. Adding lemon sorbet makes it more interesting.

Serving Size: 4

Ingredients:

- 1 cup corn starch
- 1 drop of yellow food color
- ½ cup lemon sorbet
- 1/4 cup sugar
- 3/4 cup sweet rice flour

Instruction

In a bowl, mix the sugar and rice flour.

Add the corn flour and mix well.

Add the lemon sorbet and yellow food color.

Mix well. Add to your ice cream holder.

Freeze for 4 hours. Serve.

Red Bean Paste Mochi or Daifuku Mochi

Red bean paste is commonly known as Azuki in Japan. Mochi tastes quite good when azuki is added to it.

Serving Size: 2

Cooking Time: 20 Minutes

Ingredients:

- 1 cup rice flour
- 1 cup warm water
- 1 tablespoon sugar
- 1 pinch of salt
- ½ cup Red Bean Paste or azuki
- Potato Starch to dusting

Instruction

In a microwave safe bowl, combine the warm water and rice flour.

Add the sugar and salt to it. Stir until it dissolves.

Cook in the micro oven for 1 minute. Stir once and cook for another minute.

Knead the red bean paste and make small balls.

Divide the dough into small balls too.

Roll out each dough ball and stuff the red bean paste ball inside. Seal from all sides with the dough. Repeat the process with all. Use potato starch if needed to reduce the stickiness of the balls.

Yaki Mochi or Grilled Rice Cake

The idea of grilled mochi is exciting in itself. Japanese love these grilled taste of rice cakes.

Serving Size: 2

Cooking Time: 10 Minutes

Ingredients:

- 1 cup rice flour
- 1 cup warm water
- 1 tablespoon brown sugar
- 1 pinch of cinnamon powder
- 1 pinch of nutmeg powder
- Oil for grilling

Instruction

Combine the warm water with brown sugar. Stir until the sugar dissolves.

Add the rice flour and stir until well combined.

Add the cinnamon and nutmeg and mix well.

Create square or round shapes. Add oil to the grate of the grilling machine.

Grill the mochi carefully from both sides.

Serve.

Warabi Mochi

This mochi is made from warabi starch flour. It is not always available around the world. If you want to make it and cannot find this flour, you can substitute it with potato starch flour.

Serving Size: 2

Ingredients:

- 1 cup warabi starch flour
- ½ cup warm water
- 1 pinch salt
- 1 pinch cinnamon
- ½ cup brown sugar

Instruction

In a large bowl, mix the warm water with the brown sugar.

Add cinnamon and salt and stir well.

Add the warabi starch flour.

Mix until it is well combined.

Create little balls or squares and roll them onto more flour to prevent the stickiness.

Serve.

Mochi Crepe

This is a unique way to make crepe the mochi style. I have used red bean paste for the spread. You can use any spread of your choice.

Serving Size: 2

Cooking Time: 5 Minutes

Ingredients:

- 1 cup rice flour
- 1 tbsp sugar
- ½ cup warm water
- 2 matcha Powder
- 4 tbsp red bean paste

Instruction

Combine the warm water with the sugar.

Add the rice flour and matcha powder.

Mix well and make dough. Divide into small balls.

Roll out each ball. Fry them from both sides for 1 minute.

Spread the red bean paste and fold them. Serve.

Milk Kuzu Mochi

Japanese love their 'Kuzu Mochi'. It is a hit amongst kids and adults. You can easily substitute the kuzu flour with Tapioca flour if you cannot get your hands on the earlier!

Serving Size: 2

Cooking Time: 2 Minutes

Ingredients:

- 1 cup kuzu flour
- 2 cup milk
- 4 tbsp sugar
- A pinch salt
- Ground nuts, to serve
- 2 tbsp dark brown sugar syrup, to serve

Instruction

In a microwave, add the milk with sugar packed in a safe bowl.

Whisk until it dissolves. Add the salt and flour.

Mix until it is well combined.

Add to the micro oven and cook for 1 minute.

Stir and cook for another minute.

Place onto a square tray and wait for it to cool down.

Cut into squares. Serve with dark brown sugar syrup and ground nuts.

Matcha (Green Tea) Warabi Mochi

This mochi is quite similar to the warabi mochi but it has matcha powder in it. Because of adding the matcha, the health value of this mochi is better.

Serving Size: 2

Cooking Time: 10 Minutes

Ingredients:

- 1 cup warabi flour
- 3 tbsp matcha powder
- ½ cup warm water
- ½ cup sugar
- A pinch of sea salt

Instruction

Combine the warm water with salt and sugar.

Mix well. Add the matcha powder and warabi flour.

Mix until everything is well mixed.

Steam the mixture for 10 minutes.

Let it cool down a bit and create balls.

Roll them onto more matcha powder. Serve.

Pan Fried Savory Mochi

you would not believe how good this tastes unless you try it out yourself. Adding the egg makes it softer.

Serving Size: 4

Cooking Time: 10 Minutes

Ingredients:

- 1 radish, peeled, chopped
- 1 cup Rice Flour
- ½ cup Sweet Rice Flour
- ¼ cup water
- Salt to taste
- 4 tbsp Dried Shrimp, chopped
- Fresh coriander, chopped
- Pepper to taste
- 1 egg
- 2 green chilies, chopped
- Oil for frying

Instruction

Combine the flours and salt together.

Add the dried shrimp, chili, coriander, salt and pepper.

Add the water and make dough.

Create small patties. Fry them golden brown from both sides.

Serve hot.

Raspberry Mochi

Raspberry and rice flour or any other gluttonous flour goes quite well. It brings out the authentic flavors of raspberries in the form of a dainty delight.

Serving Size: 2

Cooking Time: 10 Minutes

Ingredients:

1 cup tapioca flour

- A pinch of nutmeg
- A pinch of salt
- ½ cup honey
- ½ cup raspberry juice

Instruction

In a bowl, combine all the ingredients.

Mix well and knead into small balls.

Place into a steamer. Steam them for about 10 minutes.

Dust flour if require reducing the stickiness.

Daifuku Mandarin Mochi

This mochi looks ravishing when you cut it open in half. This can be a great crowd favorite.

Serving Size: 2

Cooking Time: 5 Minutes

Ingredients:

- 1 cup tapioca flour
- A pinch of nutmeg
- A pinch of salt
- ½ cup warm water
- 4-5 mandarins

Instruction

In a bowl combine the tapioca flour with salt and nutmeg.

Add the warm water and create dough.

Divide the dough into 4 balls. Roll them out flat.

Carefully add each mandarin into each flat piece.

Seal the edges carefully. Steam them for 5 minutes only. Serve.

Honey Glazed Fried Mochi Balls

Fried mochi tastes great and when you add a honey glaze to it, it elevates the final taste of the dish.

Serving Size: 2

Cooking Time: 10 Minutes

Ingredients:

- 1 cup tapioca flour
- ½ cup rice flour
- ½ cup Water
- A pinch of nutmeg
- A pinch of cinnamon
- A pinch of salt
- ½ cup honey
- 1 tsp lemon juice
- Oil for frying

Instruction

Combine the honey and lemon juice. Heat it up and set aside for now.

In a bowl combine the flours with spices and salt.

Add the water and make dough. Create bite size balls.

Fry them golden brown. Drizzle the honey glaze and serve.

Fried Cheesy Mochi

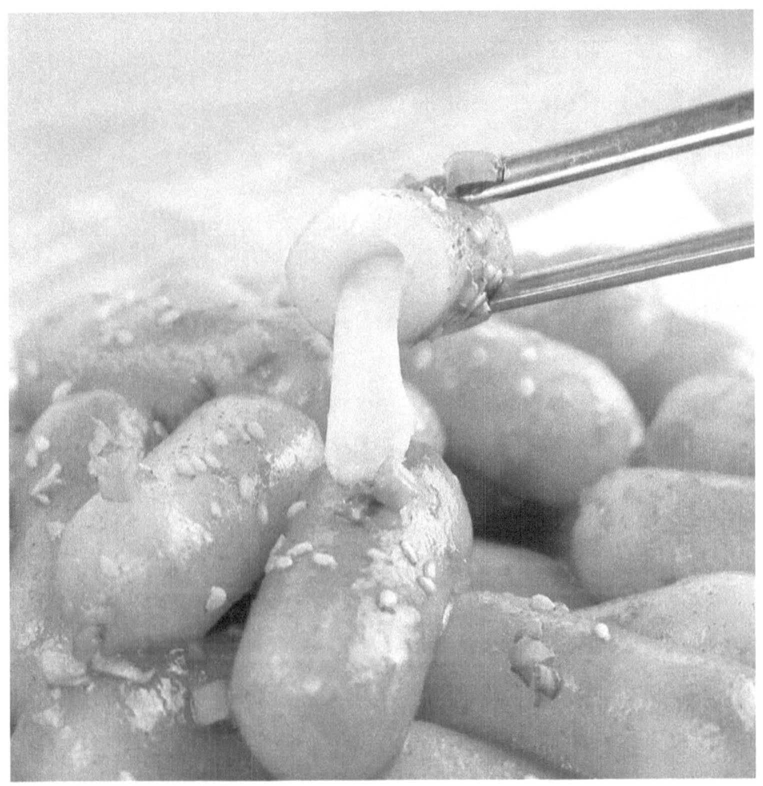

Fried mochi is good and you know what is even better? Cheery mochi! With each bite, you get woozy cheese.

Serving Size: 2

Cooking Time: 10 Minutes

Ingredients:

- 1 cup rice flour
- 1/3 cup water
- ½ cup cheese cubes
- A pinch of salt
- Oil for frying

Instruction

Combine the flour with salt and water. Make dough.

Divide into 8-10 balls. Roll them flat. Add one cheese cube into each flat tortilla and seal the edges.

Fry them golden brown. Serve hot.

Banana Mochi

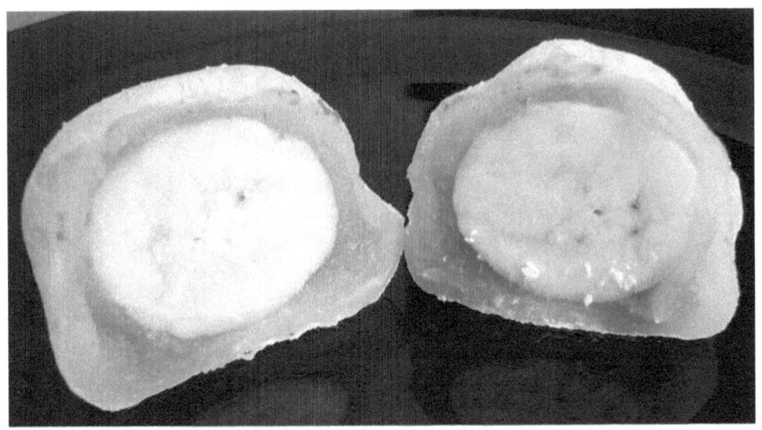

You get a slice of fresh banana in each mochi. This recipe works best with semi ripe banana. It the banana is too mushy; it will not hold its shape.

Serving Size: 2

Cooking Time: 10 Minutes

Ingredients:

- 1 cup tapioca flour
- 1 banana, cut into thick slices
- ½ cup warm water
- A pinch of sugar
- A pinch of cinnamon

Instruction

Combine the tapioca flour, sugar and cinnamon.

Add the warm water and create dough.

Divide it into 8 sections and roll them out flat. Make a pocket and add banana slice.

Seal the edge and form a ball shape.

Steam the balls for 10 minutes. Serve.

Blueberry Mochi Cake

Mochi cake with fresh blueberries tastes heavenly. You can add any fruit of your choice here.

Serving Size: 4

Cooking Time: 20 Minutes

Ingredients:

- 1 cup rice flour
- 2 tbsp corn flour
- 1 cup sugar
- 2 eggs
- 1 cup butter
- 1 cup fresh blueberries
- 1 tsp baking powder
- 1 tsp baking soda
- 1 drop vanilla essence

Instruction

Preheat to 350 degrees F of the oven. Add parchment paper on the bottom part of the cake pan.

In a bowl whisk the eggs for 2 minutes.

Add the sugar and beat for 3 minutes.

Add the butter and beat for 2 minutes.

Add the vanilla essence and mix.

Add the dry ingredients and fold them gently.

Add the blueberries and mix. Add to a cake pan.

Bake for 20 minutes. Serve in room temperature.

Mochi Pancake

Did you know you can make mochi pancakes too? This one has strawberry flavors in it.

Serving Size: 2

Cooking Time: 10 Minutes

Ingredients:

- 1 cup tapioca flour
- 2 tbsp strawberry compote
- Fresh strawberries to serve
- 2 tbsp corn flour
- Honey to serve
- 2 tbsp butter
- 1 egg
- ½ tsp baking powder
- ½ cup warm milk
- A drop of strawberry extract

Instruction

In a mixing bowl, whisk the egg with strawberry compote.

Add the butter and milk. Whisk until well mixed.

Add the dry ingredients and fold in.

Fry the pancakes golden brown.

Serve with strawberry slices and honey on top.

Strawberry Mochi

Strawberry really complements mochi treats. Adding a slice of fresh strawberry gives the mochi treat a fresh vibe. Add a drop of pink color for the outer layer and it will look visually stimulating.

Serving Size: 2

Cooking Time: 10 Minutes

Ingredients:

- 1 cup tapioca flour
- 2 tbsp coconut flour
- ½ cup halved fresh strawberries
- 2 tbsp agave nectar
- ½ cup warm water
- A drop of pink food color
- A pinch of cinnamon

Instructions

Combine the tapioca flour, coconut flour, agave nectar, warm water and cinnamon.

Add food color and mix well. Divide it into 8 little balls.

Flatten each ball and put one strawberry piece in the middle. Seal from all sides.

Steam the mochi strawberry balls for 10 minutes. Serve.

Pumpkin Mochi

You can make your mochi slightly healthy by adding pumpkin puree to it. It surprisingly tastes quite good.

Serving Size: 2

Cooking Time: 10 Minutes

Ingredients:

- 1 cup potato starch
- 2 tbsp corn flour
- 1 tbsp rice flour
- ½ cup pumpkin puree
- ½ cup warm water
- 4 tbsp honey
- A pinch of nutmeg
- A pinch of clove
- A pinch of cinnamon

Instruction

Combine all the ingredients and knead using your hands.

Make little balls. Add them to the steamer.

Steam them for 10 minutes. Serve.

Peanut and Coconut Mochi

Peanuts are really good for our brain health. It is one of the good fats you need for our body and skin. This mochi is a powerhouse of flavors and nutrition with coconut and peanuts.

Serving Size: 2

Cooking Time: 20 Minutes

Ingredients:

- 1 cup rice flour
- 2 tbsp corn flour
- 4 tbsp sugar
- 1 cup coconut milk
- 2 tbsp coconut oil
- 1 cup chopped peanuts
- ½ cup shredded coconut
- 2 tbsp sugar
- 1 tbsp butter
- Desiccated coconut for dusting

Instruction

In a pan melt the butter. Add the shredded coconut with sugar.

Toss for 5 minutes. Add the chopped peanuts. Toss for 2 minutes and turn off the heat. Create little balls using the mixture.

In a bowl combine the rice flour, corn flour, honey, coconut oil and coconut milk.

Make dough and knead well. Divide into 10 balls. Flatten each ball and add coconut peanut ball in the middle of each.

Seal from all corners and repeat with all 10 of them.

Steam them for 10 minutes. Coat them onto desiccated coconut. Serve.

Matcha Mochi Pancake

Start your breakfast with a healthy note with this matcha mochi pancake. It is quite the same as regular pancakes but the ingredients are what make it healthy.

Serving Size: 2

Cooking Time: 10 Minutes

Ingredients:

- 1 cup glutinous tapioca flour
- A pinch of salt
- 4 tbsp sugar
- ½ cup milk
- 2 tbsp rice flour
- ¼ cup matcha powder
- 2 tbsp butter
- 1 tbsp honey, to serve
- 1 tbsp white chocolate chips, to serve

Instruction

Combine the matcha powder with salt, tapioca flour and rice flour.

Add the butter, milk and sugar to it. Whisk until it is smooth.

Fry them golden brown in batches.

Serve hot with chocolate chips and honey on top.

Green Tea Coconut Mochi

This particular mochi balls not only tastes good but also looks very presentable. It has good health value too because of the matcha powder.

Serving Size: 2

Cooking Time: 10 Minutes

Ingredients:

- ¼ cup white bean paste
- 1 tsp matcha powder
- 2 tbsp rice flour
- 1/3 cup sugar
- 1 cup coconut flour
- A pinch of salt
- ½ cup warm water

Instruction

Combine the matcha powder, sugar, rice flour and white bean paste. Mix well. Create little balls.

Combine the warm water with salt and coconut flour. Mix well and knead using hands.

Divide into 6-8 balls. Roll out the ball and stuff each with the white bean matcha ball.

Seal the edges carefully. Steam them for 10 minutes. Serve.

Mochi Fig Pancake

Mochi pancakes do have a unique texture to them. Adding figs adds another layer of deliciousness to this breakfast recipe.

Serving Size: 2

Cooking Time: 10 Minutes

Ingredients:

- 1 cup glutinous rice flour
- 2 tbsp corn flour
- ¼ cup fig compote
- 1 tbsp honey, to serve
- ¼ cup diced fresh figs to serve
- 2 tbsp butter
- ½ cup milk
- A pinch of salt

Instruction

Combine the corn flour with rice flour.

Add the butter, milk and mix well.

Add the fig compote and salt. Mix well.

In a nonstick pan, fry the pancakes golden brown.

Serve hot with honey and fresh figs on top.

Green Tea Mochi Cake Recipe

Have you ever tried green tea mochi cakes? They surprisingly taste quite good and have a chewy texture to it.

Serving Size: 2

Cooking Time: 20 Minutes

Ingredients:

- 1 cup tapioca flour
- 2 tbsp rice flour
- ½ cup sugar
- 1 egg
- 1 tsp baking powder
- ½ cup coconut milk
- 1 pinch of salt
- 4 tbsp matcha powder

Instruction

Combine the matcha powder, salt, baking powder and flours.

In a bowl, whisk the egg. Add sugar and beat well.

Add the coconut milk and mix again.

Add the dry ingredients and lightly fold in.

Pour into your cake pan. Bake for 20 minutes with 350 degrees F.

Serve in room temperature.

Peach Mochi

Peach mochi looks so soothing to the eyes. The color itself is calming.

Serving Size: 2

Cooking Time: 10 Minutes

Ingredients:

- 1 cup glutinous rice flour
- ½ cup peach juice
- ¼ cup agave nectar
- Confectioner's sugar for dusting

Instruction

In a bowl combine the rice flour with the peach juice.

Add the agave nectar and mix well.

Create little balls using your hands. Steam them for 10 minutes.

Roll them on confectioner's sugar. Serve.

Conclusion

Japanese cuisine is filled with interesting and unique dishes that people from around the world do not eat in regular basis. But if you are a foodie and have fun in the kitchen, you must not miss out on this traditional Japanese sweet treats. The variation is impressive. Everyone would find something they love in these 30 mochi recipes. The art of making mochi is fairly simple. You would not know how easy it is to make them unless you try it yourself.

Author's Afterthoughts

Thanks ever so much to each of my cherished readers for investing the time to read this book!

I know you could have picked from many other books, but you chose this one. So, a big thanks for downloading this book and reading all the way to the end.

If you enjoyed this book or received value from it, I'd like to ask you for a favor. Please take a few minutes to post an honest and heartfelt review on Amazon.com. Your support does make a difference and helps to benefit other people.

Thanks for your Reviews!

Rachael Rayner

9 798609 523334